THE
FLEET AIR ARM
IN FOCUS

PART TWO

£8.95

FLEET AIR ARM

MUSEUM

One of the world's largest aviation museums with over forty historic aircraft on display including Concorde 002. Many unique displays and exhibitions tell the story of naval aviation from 1908 to the present day. Five major new attractions opened recently and include the Harrier Jump Jet Story and the Underwater Experience. Other attractions include World War I, World War II, The Falklands Islands Conflict, the Women's Royal Naval Service and the Japanese Kamikaze Bombers. Plus Airfield Viewing Galleries, Super X Simulator, Open Cockpits and a Children's Aviation Adventure Playground. Free car park, picnic areas.
Coaches and caravans welcome.

Gift shop and licensed restaurant. Open all year daily except 24th, 25th and 26th December from 10.00 a.m. to 5.30 p.m. (4.30 p.m. in winter).

Royal Naval Air Station
Yeovilton, Somerset, BA22 8HT.
Telephone:
Ilchester (0935) 840565.
Just off the A303/A37 on the B3151 near Ilchester.

This is not a history but an attempt to capture something of the spirit of the Fleet Air Arm through photographs. The majority come from the Fleet Air Arm Museum and my special thanks go to Len Lovell (until recently on the staff) and Graham Mottram who gave permission for me to use them. Others were provided by Brian Beer, Geoffrey David, Bob Duke, John Hayman, Antony Pearce and Captain RCV Ross RN (Ret'd). The book was made possible by my wife Jandy and son Andrew who typed, helped and encouraged.

SWORDFISH I Torpedo Spotter Reconnaissance Aircraft overfly HMS GLORIOUS whilst serving with the Mediterranean Fleet in 1937. The nearer aircraft are from 812 Squadron; those furthest away, with the dark tailplanes, are from 823 Squadron. All the aircraft are from the first SWORDFISH production batch.

SWORDFISH I aircraft of 812 Squadron in close formation photographed by the observer in the lead aircraft. The aircraft in the foreground is in the number 3 position and is fitted with light series bomb carriers under the lower mainplane.

Seconds after launch. A photograph taken by the observer of a SWORDFISH over the telegraphist air gunner's head. This aircraft is probably the first to take off from a range, the remainder of which can be seen running on deck. As first off, he has had the shortest free take off run and has hardly climbed at all since leaving the deck; those behind will be more fortunate. Note the steam jet between the catapults indicating that the wind is down the deck.

Pilot's eye view of HMS GLORIOUS in 1937. He is flying down the starboard side of the ship into the "slot" position to join the visual circuit. Once clear ahead of the ship, the pilot will break to port across the bows and fly a tight visual circuit to land. At this stage, GLORIOUS had Mark III arrester gear but no barrier. On landing, each aircraft had to be struck down into the hangar leaving a clear deck for the next astern. The metal structure in the top right of the picture is a torpedo attack sight. Each knob on the horizontal bar represents 10 knots of the target ship's speed. Having estimated this, the pilot keeps the relevant knob to port or starboard on the target during his attack thus "aiming off" the torpedo sufficiently to allow it to intercept the target at the end of its run. The device was crude but resiliant and remarkably effective.

Part of the FIREFLY fuselage repair line at RNAY BELFAST on 27 May 1953. A heavily posed picture showing the civilian workforce stopping work for a moment amid their coronation decorations. The aircraft are FIREFLY AS5s.

Another part of the fuselage repair shop on 27 May 1953. Wing centre sections, visible in the foreground, are being mated with FIREFLY fuselages and undercarriages. The aircraft at the back of the picture has had the engine bearers mounted on the engine bulkhead.

One of the three prototype SUPERMARINE SEAGULL ASR1s seconds before taking a wire during carrier trials on HMS ILLUS-TRIOUS in October 1949. With large numbers of older seaplanes available and helicopter development progressing rapidly, the type was not ordered into production despite the success of the trials.

FIREFLY FR1s over HMS ILLUSTRIOUS in 1949. The Carrier is into wind with the deck clear ready to recover them. The photograph was taken by the observer in the leading aircraft. The 2 in the side number painted on the aircraft indicated, at that time, a two-seater. The remaining two digits indicated the individual aircraft. The pod under the aircraft is an air/surface radar scanner.

A BLACKBURN YB1 during carrier trials on HMS ILLUSTRIOUS in 1950. The type was produced to meet the same specification as the FAIREY GANNET, but only the GANNET went into production.

A Dutch SEA FURY Mark 50 seen after coming to grief on the barrier of HMS ILLUSTRIOUS. The risk of fire has been reduced by the amount of foam covering the engine and the deck. An officer from the Air Engineering Department is guiding Jumbo the crane forward to start salvage operations.

Barrier prang by a SEA FURY Mark 50 of the Dutch Navy on HMS ILLUSTRIOUS. The Pilot has leapt clear of the wreck on the port side, unfortunately just as a flash fire breaks out from the volatile Avgas spilling onto the deck past the hot engine.

A MARTINET from a Fleet Requirements Unit about to drop a sleeve target on the flight deck of HMS VENGEANCE during a work-up. MARTINETS formed part of the equipment of no less than 20 second line squadrons before their retirement in the early 1950s. On training sorties such as these, fighter pilots fired painted rounds so that an individual's score could be deduced from the colour of the holes (or lack of them) in the sleeve once it was dropped back on deck.

A SEA HORNET NF21 of 809 Squadron seconds before taking a wire on HMS EAGLE.

A STURGEON TT2 of 728 Fleet Requirements Squadron lands on a light fleet carrier of the Mediterranean Fleet. The LSO (who has his windbreak lowered) is about to give the pilot the 'cut' signal.

The Coronation Naval Review, Spithead, 15 June 1953. HMCS MAGNIFICENT is seen anchored beyond the sailing ship AMERI-GO VESPUCCI. Visible beyond MAGNIFICENT are the Indian cruiser DELHI, the New Zealand cruiser BLACK PRINCE and the destroyers BARROSA and AISNE.

An aerial view of the Coronation Review, 1953. It must have been one of the largest ever assemblies of British carriers. Visible in this picture, from the foreground, are EAGLE, INDOMITABLE, IMPLACABLE, INDEFATIGABLE, ILLUSTRIOUS, THESEUS, MAGNIFICENT (RCN), SYDNEY (RAN) and the maintenance carrier PERSEUS.

HMS EAGLE shortly after joining the Fleet in 1952. The 13th Carrier Air Group had left TRIUMPH by this stage and re- equipped for service in EAGLE. Visible here are ATTACKER F1s of 800 and 803 Squadrons and FIREFLY AS6s of 812 and 814 Squadrons. Though not visible here, the remainder of the Air Group consisted of the FIREBRAND TF5s of 827 Squadron. Flag "Foxtrot" is 'at the dip' indicating that flying operations are about to take place, borne out by the fact that whilst the FIREFLIES have not yet started, marshallers are in place ready for them to do so. Three groundcrew are catching a few minutes rest on the round-down aft, out of sight of authority. The FIREFLIES on the port and starboard quarter spots have their out-board wings folded still since spreading is a manual process and the squadron maintain-ers cannot yet get at them.

A storm range. FIREFLY AS6s and a SKYRAIDER AEW1 spread and firmly lashed down to minimise damage as HMS EAGLE heads into a storm.

One of EAGLE's FIREFLY AS6s has landed heavily whilst operating in stormy conditions. The hook has taken number 1 wire whilst number 4 has been snagged by the radome under the starboard wing as it is dragged along the deck. The impact has proved too much for the starboard oleo which is flying over the starboard wing!

Goofers in the island crane forward to see the action as the flight deck crew rush toward the aircraft. A hose has been run out with its attendant drum of foam making compound. Firesuitmen with first-aid fire-fighting appliances have already reached the cockpit area and are helping the crew to get out. The LSO (not visible behind his windbreak) has waved-off the next aircraft which is overshooting to port. It will be instructed by radio to raise its undercarriage and fly for endurance until the deck is clear again and ready to resume the land on.

Slings have been attached to the FIREFLY and Jumbo the crane is lifting it clear. Once it is forward of the barrier, the recovery will re-commence.

One of HMS EAGLE's ATTACKER F1s about to start. An external battery is connected to the aircraft and a first-aid fire extinguisher is close at hand aft. The pilot is looking down in the cockpit whilst carrying out his pre-start vital actions.

Supermarine ATTACKER FB2 of 803 Squadron on the flight deck of HMS EAGLE in Gibraltar. Rocket rails are fitted under the wings and a catapult launch strop has been hooked on ready for the next launch. Note the huge 250 gallon drop tank under the belly and the neat footstep extended just aft of the port intake. Several panels have been removed and the lashings in the foreground taken off so, with a maintainer in the cockpit to act as a brake number, the aircraft looks as if it is about to be struck down into the hangar. EAGLE is anchored in Algeciras Bay and those with sharp eyes might just make out HMS VANGUARD alongside the south mole in Gibraltar. The picture was taken during the combined Home and Mediterranean Fleet exercises in early 1953.

For many years a seaplane base in its own right, in 1957 when this photograph was taken, KALAFRANA formed part of HMS FALCON, RNAS HAL FAR, Malta GC. The WRNS accomodation is visible to the far right.

A brand new SEA VENOM FAW 21 from the Naval Aircraft Storage Unit at RNAS HAL FAR being conveyed by motorised lighter from Kalafrana for issue to a carrier moored in Grand Harbour in the summer of 1957. Note the pristine condition of the aircraft and the absence of any squadron codes or badges.

A FIREBRAND TF4, surplus to requirements, has been stripped of everything useful and is seen being ditched over the side of HMS ALBION suspended beneath the port side crane.

A SEA FURY FB11 of 802 Squadron has
failed to take a wire on HMS VENGEANCE and
has crashed into the after barrier dragging it forward
over the forward barrier which was in the down position.
The aircraft has only just come to rest and flight deck per-
sonnel are rushing forward with fire-fighting equipment.

A SEA HORNET NF21 has suffered a collapse of the starboard oleo. Foam is being sprayed onto the damaged starboard engine (the port looks as if it had been shut down normally). The flight deck officer is taking firm charge of the situation to the right of the picture whilst the handler to the left connects the spill of a foam making nozzle to a canister of foam making chemicals.

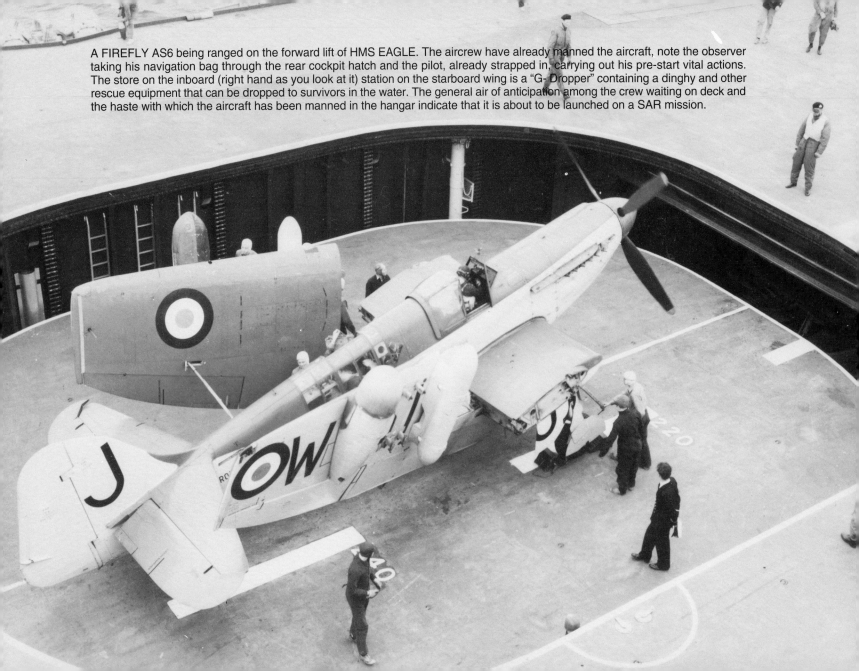

A FIREFLY AS6 being ranged on the forward lift of HMS EAGLE. The aircrew have already manned the aircraft, note the observer taking his navigation bag through the rear cockpit hatch and the pilot, already strapped in, carrying out his pre-start vital actions. The store on the inboard (right hand as you look at it) station on the starboard wing is a "G- Dropper" containing a dinghy and other rescue equipment that can be dropped to survivors in the water. The general air of anticipation among the crew waiting on deck and the haste with which the aircraft has been manned in the hangar indicate that it is about to be launched on a SAR mission.

A SEA FURY FB11 of 810 Squadron passing over the round-down of HMS CENTAUR. The LSO has just given the "cut" signal with his bats. The aircraft has a 'hung up' 25 lb. rocket on the starboard outer pylon and one has to say that the standard of protective clothing of the LSO and his assistant is remarkably casual. This was a period of transition typefied by CENTAUR's air group which included both jet and piston powered fighters operating from a ship recently fitted with an angled deck.

Lined up LEFT! One of 810 Squadron's SEA FURIES takes a wire on HMS CENTAUR, but it is well to left of the runway centreline, indeed, the port wheel is left of the left marker line of the runway. The LSO and his assistant are both concerned and have turned to follow the aircraft's progress.

The aircraft is being brought to a halt by the wire but has veered even further to the left and the port wheel has hit the spurnwater at the deck edge. The pilot fears the worst and has his head braced back against the headrest!

Too late the aircraft has come to a halt but the port oleo has gone into the catwalk and the propellors have hit the deck edge stopping, and no doubt shock loading, the engine. Note the marshaller to the left of the picture who is optimistically giving the pilot the "brakes on" signal.

Incident over. Thankfully there has been no fire and the hoses are being re-stowed. A first aid extinguisher is kept near the engine however just on case. The next move will be to get Jumbo the crane to remove the wreck.

A BARRACUDA TR3 of 815 Squadron rolls forward for a free take off from HMS INDOMITABLE. BARRACUDAS remained in limited front line service until 1953 on anti-submarine duties. In the background is a running range of SEA HORNET NF21s amd FIREFLY AS6s.

HMS CENTAUR was completed in September 1953 largely to the original 1943 design with an axial flight deck and heavy close range battery on sponsons down the port side.

As soon as HMS CENTAUR completed trials, she was taken in hand in Portsmouth Dockyard for the installation of an interim 5 degree angled deck. This involved re-working the arrester wires to lie athwart the new landing area and a small structural extension to port which led to the removal of many of the anti-aircraft weapons on the post side. She is seen here alongside Middle Slip Jetty in Portsmouth.

HMS UNICORN postwar. She was used throughout the Korean War to ferry replacement aircraft for the commonwealth carriers operating off the west coast of Korea. Visible here is the pronounced overhang at the stern; a lighter was kept under this and could be used to move aircraft from shore to ship or ship to ship. Despite her undoubted value and oustanding aircraft maintenance facilities, UNICORN paid off late in 1953 and was broken up in 1959.

A SEA VAMPIRE F20 leaving USS ANTIETAM, the first carrier in the world to be fitted with an angled deck. Trials had been carried out in 1952 with an angled deck painted on HMS TRIUMPH. These proved so successful that the US Navy went ahead and modified ANTIETAM immediately in New York Navy Yard. She visited the UK in July 1953 as part of her trials programme and operated ATTACKERS, SEA HAWKS, METEORS, SEA VAMPIRES, SEA VENOMS and WYVERNS. HMS CENTAUR was to be the first British Carrier to be modified with an angled deck.

A DRAGONFLY HR3 of RNAS LOSSIEMOUTH Station Flight carrying out a winch check prior to take off. DRAGONFLIES were the first robust, practical helicopters to serve with the fleet and equipped a number of SAR Flights in carriers and air stations throughout the 1950s.

A Sikorsky WHIRLWIND HAS22 winching a senior officer from the forecastle of a BAY class frigate whilst a second WHIRLWIND stands by in case of problems. There is very little natural wind, and so the ship is steaming briskly into what little there is to provide the helicopter pilot with a good wind over deck to ease the power required to hover. The serial number makes it likely that this was one of a batch of WHIRLWIND 22s issued to 845 Squadron in 1954 to evaluate and advance the role of the helicopter in anti-submarine warfare.

The SEAMEW AS1 was designed to be a simple, easily operated and cheap anti-submarine aircraft for potential use from escort carriers in wartime; very much in the SWORDFISH tradition. It is seen here taking part in carrier trials on HMS WARRIOR. 3 Prototypes and 25 production examples were built but the type fell victim to the 1957 Defence Review and production was terminated. The SEAMEW never equipped a front line unit.

A SEAHAWK FGA6 of 804 Squadron on the port catapult of HMS ARK ROYAL . Flag FOXTROT is close up and launch operations are in full swing. The aircraft is held back by automatic chocks (which will be lowered flush with the deck before launch) the holdback is connected and two Flight Deck Engineers, known as badgers because of their black and white surcoats, have connected the launching strop and are holding it in place. The leading badger (arm and leg visible at the left of picture) gives the order to the catapult operator to move the shuttle forward to tension the strop. The jet blast deflector is not yet raised behind the catapult and a further SEAHAWK is visible awaiting its turn to launch. Overhead, two SEAHAWKS can be seen orbiting the ship in the low wait pattern. They are watching the deck and preparing to slot into the landing circuit as soon as the launch is complete. Note the 804 Squadron badge of a tiger's head holding a dagger. The Squadron motto was "swift to kill".

Two SEAHAWK FB3s of 897 Squadron orbit HMS EAGLE in the low wait pattern. A launch is still underway on deck with SEA-HAWKS and SEA VENOMS moving towards the catapults. Unusually the SAR WHIRLWIND is to starboard of the carrier; a more normal position would be to port. The returning aircraft will have been given a "Charlie" time(the moment their wheels are due to hit the deck) and they will thus be keen to set themselves up to slot into the landing circuit at just the right moment. 897's badge was a Caspian Tern's head visible on the nose of aircraft 457. Beneath the badge, smoke staining indicates that the aircraft's guns have been fired during the sortie.

Lined up right! A WYVERN S4 of 831 Squadron has successfully taken number 1 wire on HMS ARK ROYAL but lined up right of the angled deck centreline. On coming to a halt it veered right and hit a SEAHWAK of 804 Squadron. The incident took place on 22 February 1957.

An overhead view of the previous deck landing incident. The use of fuel with a higher flash point in jet turbo-prop engines (known to the RN as AVCAT) has drastically reduced the risk of a fire but firefighting equipment is readily to hand just in case. The usual crowd has gathered to investigate the damage and work out methods of prizing the two aircraft apart. At bottom left the wire has been disengaged from the aircraft hook, and at top right a flight deck tractor stands ready.

During the mid 1950s Pilotless Target Aircraft were procured from the French company SFEC-MAS (Societe Francaise d'Etudes et de Construction de Materiels Speciaux). These were based on the wartime German V1 flying bombs but incorporated many detail improvements. Performance varied but typically they were capable of 280 knots at 10,000 feet for 40 minutes. They were very much superior to the more conventional targets towed behind aircraft such as the STURGEON and few, if any, were destroyed by the guns of the Mediterranean Fleet. The PTA is seen here being assembled on the launching ramp above Hassan's Cave on Benghaisa Point at the end of Marsaxlokk.

PTA Launch. In flight the little aircraft was radio controlled and constant thrust from the motor was achieved by an automatic fuel regulator. It could operate between 2000 and 20,000 feet. The control station was mounted in a large vehicle which was capable of tracking the target by radar.

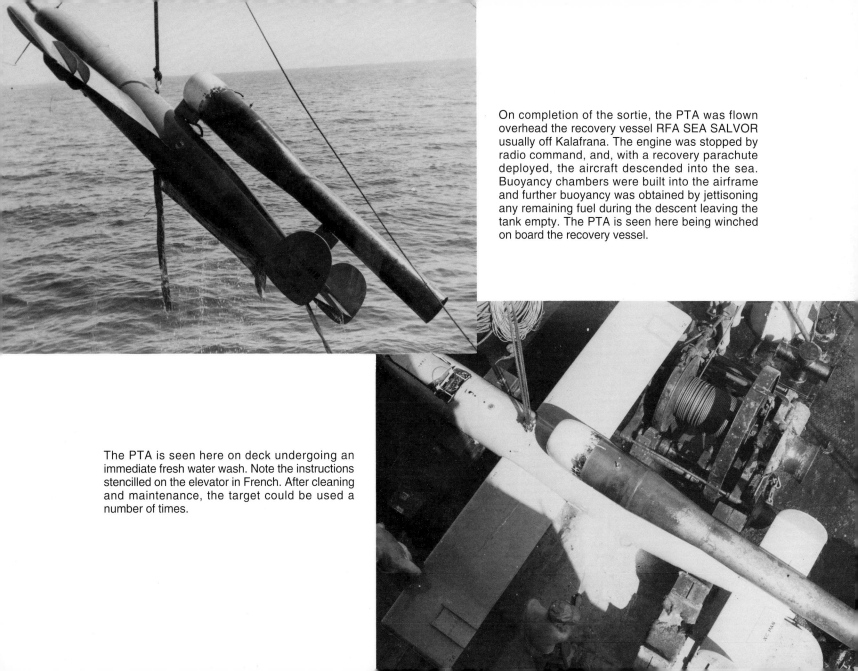

On completion of the sortie, the PTA was flown overhead the recovery vessel RFA SEA SALVOR usually off Kalafrana. The engine was stopped by radio command, and, with a recovery parachute deployed, the aircraft descended into the sea. Buoyancy chambers were built into the airframe and further buoyancy was obtained by jettisoning any remaining fuel during the descent leaving the tank empty. The PTA is seen here being winched on board the recovery vessel.

The PTA is seen here on deck undergoing an immediate fresh water wash. Note the instructions stencilled on the elevator in French. After cleaning and maintenance, the target could be used a number of times.

A SKYRAIDER AEW1 of 849 A Flight carries out a missed approach flying with wheels, flaps and hook down, low and slow down the port side of HMS EAGLE. As normal with propeller driven aircraft, the pilot has his canopy open so that he can make a rapid exit in an emergency. the advent of the ejection seat, which could punch the pilot through the perspex, made this precaution unnecessary and indeed dangerous. If the canopy slid forward half way through an ejection it could kill the hapless pilot.

A GANNET AS1 leaves HMS EAGLE's port catapult in June 1956. The wire launching strop is visible falling away beyond the deck edge as the aircraft climbs away. At the time they cost £15 each and one was lost with every aircraft launched. The GANNET was not fitted with ejection seats and all three crew members have opened their canopies in case the aircraft ditches and they have to clamber out in a hurry! The handler on the left, by the 100 foot marker, appears to have been knocked over backwards by the aircraft's launch. The other aircraft on deck are SEAHAWKS.

A SEAHAWK FGA6 of 800 Squadron takes number 1 wire on HMS ALBION in 1957. The SEAHAWK was a good deck landing aircraft.

GANNETs of 826 Squadron carry out a near perfect recovery. HMS EAGLE has just steadied into wind as the first aircraft rolls its wings level, nicely lined up on the centreline, height just right to take the target wire. The pilot is flying the "meatball" on the mirror sight. The second aircraft is backing up the first well, aiming to give him just long enough to fold and clear the angled deck before he too plucks a wire. The carrier is vulnerable to torpedo attack while she steams steadily into wind for launch and recovery. These aircraft are giving a perfect demonstration of how to minimise that time. The interval between the two GANNETS should be about 45 seconds to give the wire caught by the leader time to reset.

HMS ALBION, 30 August 1958. This SEAHAWK FGA6 of 804 Squadron has had its chocks removed in error before the engine has started. The Ship's motion has caused it to roll backwards into the port mirror sight, damaging both itself and the sight. Note the broken drop tank under the starboard wing and the teams of handlers running in with foam hoses in case there is a fire. The plane-guard WHIRLWIND is in the usual station on the port beam.

A SEAHAWK FGA6 of 804 Squadron has dropped low on the approach and hit the round-down collapsing the port oleo. Fortunately it ran forward and engaged number 1 wire which brought the aircraft to a halt, more or less on the centreline. Look bottom left where firefighting teams are already running out hoses. The battery of 4 lights built out from the ship's side (visible above the aircraft's port wing) are the source lights for the mirror sight. A number were fitted so that failures of bulbs would not "take out" the mirror. They also had different supplies so that failure of any one was not catastrophic, the mirror sight being vital for jet recoveries.

A large team of engineers heave down on the starboard wing while others push up on the port one. This allows a wheeled trolley to be pushed under the port wing so that the aircraft can be towed clear of the landing area.

A formation of GANNET AS1s from RNAS EGLINTON, the Air Anti-Submarine Base in Northern Ireland. The photograph is taken from the observer's cockpit of a GANNET and the aircraft in the foreground is from 737 Squadron, the GANNET Training School based at Eglinton; the one in the background is from 812 Squadron, disembarked to Eglinton from HMS EAGLE. The absence of observer and aircrewman in the 737 aircraft make it highly likely that this is a formation training sortie.

A Wren air mechanic helping the pilot strap into his SEAHAWK. The aircraft is disembarked at a Naval Air Station and the map and aerial photograph in the cockpit show that it is about to go on a ground attack sortie. The pilot's helmet is an original Mark 1 "Bone Dome" as yet without vizor; hence the sunglasses.

SLIDE DOOR

TO OPEN

PULL OUT

A Wren Radio Mechanic carrying out a daily check on the radio in a DRAGONFLY Helicopter. The Pilot's "Bone Dome", a Mark 1 helmet, is tucked by the right of the seat indicating that this is an SAR mchine on standby.

Wren Air Mechanics refuelling a SEAHAWK of
898 Squadron at a Naval Air Station.

A number of trials aircraft were tested for carrier compatibility in the 1950s, this is the Bristol Type 173 carrying out deck landing trials on HMS EAGLE and attracting a large crowd of interested handlers. The helicopter was broadly similar to the Type 191 intended for large scale production as anti-submarine machines for both the RN and RCN. A developed version did ultimately see service as the BELVEDERE with the RAF.

HMS THESEUS, Suez 1956. A WHIRLWIND HAR3 of 845 Squadron lifting men of 45 Commando Royal Marines into action for what was to be the first helicopter assault in history. Further aft, beyond the firesuitmen and handlers, more marines are embarking in WHIRLWIND HAS22s. These were anti-submarine machines, but with the sonar stripped out to improve their load lifting capability. In the left foreground, equipment can be seen stacked ready to move ashore.

HMS THESEUS during the Suez action with WHIRLWINDS and SYCAMORES of the Joint Army/RAF Helicopter Development Unit which operated alongside 845 Squadron. THESEUS, together with another carrier OCEAN, had been employed as training ships before the crisis but both were hastily fitted out as Commando Carriers and performed very creditably. The later decision to convert two carriers permanently to commando helicopter support was based on the experience at Suez.

A SEA VENOM FAW21 of 893 Squadron has failed to lower its undercarriage or hook and has therefore had to recover into a nylon barrier on HMS ARK ROYAL. The advent of the angled deck did away with the need for a steel wire barrier which would stop aircraft running forward into the deck park. There was still the problem however of how to stop an aircraft that could not lower its hook. This was solved by producing a nylon barrier pack which could be rigged across the runway if the need arose. A watch of handlers could have one rigged in 4 to 5 minutes. The nylon strips acted on the wings, with the fuselage sliding through a gap thus ensuring the safety of the aircrew.

A flight deck scene on HMS BULWARK whilst with the Far East Fleet in 1958. The majority of aircraft are SEA VENOM FAW 22s of 891 Squadron, with one SEAHAWK FGA6 of 801 Squadron to the right and a SKYRAIDER AEW1 of 849 D Flight in midnight blue finish at the after end of the runway, ready for a possible free take off. Note that two of the arrester wires normally lay over the after lift and they had to be unrigged and drawn aside to allow its use. The next ship astern is HMNZS ROYALIST with two "C" class destroyers beyond her.

On 13 September 1958, the Liberian tanker MELIKA collided with the French tanker FERNAND GILABERT and caught fire. A SKYRAIDER of 849 D Flight sighted the striken ships and HMS BULWARK sped to the scene. A fire party, led by the First Lieutenant, was put onto the MELIKA by 845 Squadron's WHIRLWIND helicopters which then took badly injured seamen from both ships to the RAF Base on Masira Island. The fire took some time to extinguish, but once it was out BULWARK took MELIKA in tow to safety at Ras Al Hadd, where temporary repairs were effected by a Naval Salvage Team. They are seen here minutes after the tow was begun. For its part in the rescue, 845 Squadron was awarded the Boyd Trophy for 1958. This prize is awarded to a front line squadron for the most outstanding feat of Naval Aviation in each year.

A WYVERN S4 of 813 Squadron carries out deck landing practice on HMS EAGLE in 1957. Since it is a practice pass, the hook is raised and the pilot will hit the deck and roll for another flying circuit. The Squadron's unofficial badge "Dennis the Menace" riding a bomb labelled 813 is visible under the cockpit. The WYVERN was a turbo-prop strike aircraft that had a protracted period of development and had more than its fair share of accidents.

A WHIRLWIND HAR3 lifts off from HMS WARRIOR during Operation GRAPPLE, the nuclear test programme on Christmas Island in 1957. It has lifted directly out of the chocks, common practice for RN helicopters to prevent any tendency to slip on a moving, wet deck. It is indicative of the low rate of flying that the deck edge guardrails are permanently rigged and the outline of a deck hockey pitch has been painted on! Guardrails are even rigged around the forward lift. History does not relate the purpose of this flight but it is interesting to see that the oleos have been wrapped with plastic sheeting and openings appear to be taped closed. The helicopter is fitted with a REBECCA homing device, the aerials of which are visible just beneath the windshield.

Pilots eye view of HMS ARK ROYAL. Line up is good, but the approach is slightly low. The projector sight replaced the mirror in operational carriers from 1960 onwards. It is seen here on a prominent sponson on the port side. To fly the perfect approach, a pilot needs to concentrate on the sight to ensure that he is on the correct glide slope, keeping the projected light or "meatball" level with the green datum arms fitted on either side of the sight. If the ball goes below the datums you are low, if it goes above them you are high. Red wave-off lights are fitted above the datums and if they are flashed, it is mandatory to break off the approach and go round again. Constant reference must be made to the brightly painted centreline to ensure the correct line-up and airspeed must be monitored. To help with the latter, many naval aircraft, from the late 1950s onwards, were fitted with audio airspeed indicators in order that the pilot could keep his eyes on the sight.

SEAHAWK FGA6 fighters of 898 Squadron from HMS EAGLE in 1958. The aircraft nearest the camera sports the new extra dark sea grey and white colour scheme adopted in the late 1950s for fighters, the other two aircraft retain the older scheme. They are in VIC formation, note the two wingmen have their heads turned concentrating on the lead aircraft. The smoke stains on 476 port wing indicate that this has been a rocket firing sortie probably against a splash target towed by a warship.

Winter North Atlantic operations by HMS VICTORI-OUS after her complete reconstruction in Portsmouth Dockyard. The aircraft in the fore-ground are SCIMITAR F1s of 803 Squadron with SEA VENOM FAW22s of 893 Squadron and a sin-gle SKYRAIDER AEW1 of 849 B Flight. A launch is about to take place and the SEA VENOMS have just pressed their cartridge starters (note the pall of smoke over them). The SCIMITARS used a Palouste turbo starter which was wheeled from air-craft to aircraft and is visible by the SCIMITAR just left of the line of SEA VENOMS. Directors are already in position to move the aircraft up the deck towards the catapults for what promises to be a most unpleasant launch looking at the poor visibili-ty and falling snow!

HM Ships VICTORIOUS, ARK ROYAL and HERMES in line astern, all with SCIMITARS loaded on the catapults about to launch. Regrettably this is a sight that is unlikely to be repeated.

HMS BULWARK in the Johore Straits after her conversion to a Commando Carrier. As well as the WESSEX HU5 helicopters of 848 Squadron in this Alpha Range, she has a Royal Marines Commando with its vehicles, helicopters and attached Commando Battery, Royal Artillery together with several RAF WHIRLWINDS. Truly a joint service organisation.

HMS BULWARK coming alongside
in HM Naval Base SINGAPORE.

WHIRLWIND HAS 7 B of 848 Naval Air Squadron after a forced landing due to engine failure; a not uncommon event for the type. In flaring to reduce the impact, the rotor disc has been rotated too far aft and has severed the tail pylon.

HMS WOOLASTON is refuelled at sea from HMS BULWARK during confrontation operations off Borneo. The helicopters are WHIRLWIND HAS7s of 848 Squadron.

In 1966, HMS BULWARK was used for trials with the Hawker P1127, forerunner of the SEA HARRIER. For free take-offs, the original angled deck centre-line was re-painted on and the aircraft is seen here lining up for take off. Two airfield bowsers and two Jumbos are parked by the island. The second Jumbo having to be embarked as the helicopter crane would be incapable of lifting a damaged P1127. The bowsers contained AVCAT for the P1127 since the ship's own WHIRLWINDs ran on AVGAS.

HMS CENTAUR sailing
from Portsmouth Dockyard in
November 1963. She has
undergone limited modernisation
to enable her to operate second gen-
eration jets such as the SEA VIXEN.
The most obvious change is the lattice
foremast which supports a Type 965 radar. A
TACAN homing beacon is mounted on the top
of the mainmast. In the background, the Canadian
carrier HMCS BONAVENTURE with TRACKERS on
deck can be seen alongside Middle Slip Jetty.

HMS CENTAUR on 24 January 1964. In that month there was a mutiny by the Army in Tanganyika. Britain was asked to help but no Commando Carrier was available, thus CENTAUR displayed the inherent flexibility of carrier aviation by proceeding to Aden to pick up 45 Commando Royal Marines, 16/5 Lancers and two RAF BELVEDERE helicopters. She carried all these at high speed to Dar-es-Salaam together with her own air group. Landrovers and Ferret armoured cars can be seen to starboard forward of Fly 1. It remained possible to operate the SEA VIXENS but it would have been a squeeze! Once off Tanganyika, the military force was landed by the anti-submarine WESSEX helicopters of 815 Squadron and CENTAUR stood off with her fighters and GANNETS ready, if necessary, to support the force ashore.

A SCIMITAR F1 of 803 Squadron from HMS HERMES. The weapon underwing is a BULLPUP air to surface guided missile. Once fired, the missile was aimed toward the target by the pilot using a small control stick in the cockpit. Whilst better than having to fly over the target to drop a free fall bomb, BULLPUP suffered from the drawback that the parent aircraft still had to fly towards the target with the pilot's attention split between flying the missile and flying his aircraft. Although widely used throughout NATO, it was never completely successful in service.

A METEOR TT20 of the Fleet Requirements Unit, HURN parked outside Station Flight at RNAS YEOVILTON. Built as an NF11 for the RAF, this was one of a number of target tug conversions used by the Royal Navy worldwide.

A WESSEX HU5 of 848 Squadron overflying HMS ALBION whilst carrying a 105mm gun underslung. The WESSEX was the first helicopter in RN service able to carry practical loads such as this to support a commando assault.

HMS VICTORIOUS turning at speed during post refit trials in 1966. The aircraft forward is a BUCCANEER S2 of 801 Squadron, the first Squadron to take the type to sea. Further aft are SEA VIXEN FAW 2s of 893 Squadron and, aft of the island is a single GANNET AEW 3 of 849A Flight.

A Rolls Royce Avon 208 turbojet being changed in a SEA VIXEN FAW2 of 899 Squadron on the flight deck of HMS EAGLE.

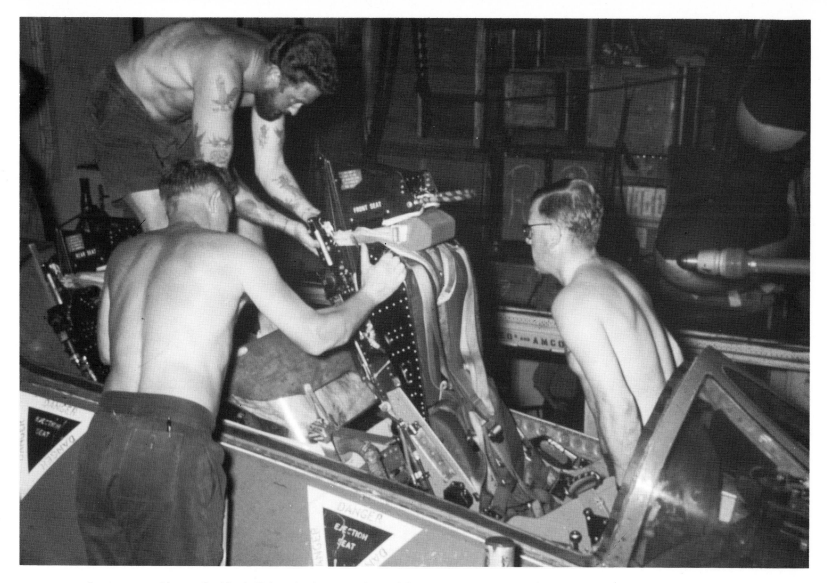

Armourers working on the Martin Baker ejection seat of a BUCCANEER S2 of 800 Squadron in the lower hangar of HMS EAGLE.

Jumbo the crane. A typical salvage crane on the flight deck of HMS EAGLE.

The Double Mamba and gearbox unit from a GANNET AEW3 of 849 D Flight in HMS EAGLE. The whole assembly could be slid forward on the yellow rails visible at bottom right to allow a change to be carried out. The hangars of carriers in the tropics reached very high temperatures, note the lack of clothing and the use of sweat rags by the maintainers.

Having removed it from the airframe, maintainers lower a Rolls Royce Avon 208 engine onto its transport cradle. The aircraft is a SEA VIXEN FAW2 of 899 Squadron in its first deployment on the newly modernised HMS EAGLE.

HMS VICTORIOUS, Far East Fleet 7 December 1964. This SEA VIXEN FAW2 of 893 Squadron failed to get its starboard undercarriage oleo to lower by either normal or emergency methods. With no shore diversion within range, the emergency nylon barrier has been rigged to ensure that the aircraft is brought safely to rest.

The SEA VIXEN takes the barrier. Unsupported by the starboard oleo the starboard wing has already fallen to the deck, shattering the empty drop tank.

The aircraft has come to rest having caught an arrester wire as well as engaging the barrier. Damage is minimal but pieces of the broken drop tank are much in evidence. The pilot leans forward in the cockpit to complete his shut-down checks.

It is now safe for the flight deck crew to move in. A fork lift truck with platform manned by firesuitmen is used to get the crew out. The observer stands on the platform while armourers make the ejection seats safe. The pilot has got out unaided and can be seen moving past the nose of the aircraft. Foam has been sprayed on the deck to lessen the chance of a spark causing a fire.

A SEA VIXEN FAW2 of 893 Squadron some minutes after making a heavy landing aboard HMS VICTORIOUS in the Indian Ocean during 1966. The crew have got out safely and the FDO is supervising the attachment of lifting slings from his standing position on the aircraft. Jumbo's jib is visible in the top left hand corner of the picture and steadying ropes are tied to the port boom and the nose oleo. The ratings in the left foreground are from the Weapon Supply Team ("bombheads") and are wearing their distinctive red and black striped flight deck jerseys.

A crowded flight deck scene on HMS VICTORIOUS with aircraft starting up for a launch. In the foreground a GANNET AEW3 of 849A Flight has a palouste starter connected although from the way both pilot and surrounding maintainers are staring at it, it appears not to be working in the expected manner. Further aft another palouste is connected to a SEA VIXEN FAW1 of 893 Squadron and yet another, much further aft is ready to start a BUCCANEER S1 of 801 Squadron. Firesuitmen with first- aid appliances move through the range ready to cope with any fire on start-up and directors are in charge of each aircraft ready to guide them forward to the catapults. Palouste starters were built in the aerodynamic shape seen here so that they could be carried underwing by a variety of aircraft and thus used for starting away from the parent carrier or base. All aircrew had thus to be proficient in their use.

"WHEELS DOWN, FLAPS DOWN, HOOK DOWN". The Landing Safety Officer's assistant checks every aircraft on finals through binoculars. This SEA VIXEN FAW1 of 892 Squadron has everything right and is photographed from the SAR helicopter seconds before taking a wire on HMS HERMES.

A SCIMITAR F1 of 800B Flight on the waist catapult of HMS EAGLE in 1964. The shuttle is moving back from the previous launch, hence all the steam escaping as it moves. Badgers are moving in to fix the strop and tension it against the shuttle whilst to the left a director moves the next aircraft forward ready to position it on the catapult as soon as the SCIMITAR has been launched. 800B Flight were used as air to air refuelling tankers to support the BUCCANEER S1s of 800 Squadron whose Gyron Junior engines were insufficiently powerful to enable them to get airborne with a heavy load of weapons and fuel. A refuelling pod can be seen under the SCIMITAR's starboard wing. The rating to the right is holding a board which states:
"CHECKS COMPLETE"..."BRAKES OFF"
a reminder shown to the pilot seconds before launch. The jet blast deflector is up ready for the launch and the black object beyond the SCIMITAR is the projector sight in the raised position so that the inboard datum arm is kept clear of taxiing wing tips.

A GANNET AEW3 of 849 A Flight at the moment of launch from HMS VICTORIOUS.

A GANNET AEW3 photographed from the planeguard helicopter seconds before landing on HMS VICTORIOUS.

A SCIMITAR F1 of 800B Flight trailing the drogue from its air to air refuelling pod whilst a BUCCANEER S1 of 800 Squadron for-
mates on it prior to topping up. Apart from the refuelling pod, the SCIMITAR carries three 200 gallon drop tanks on underwing
pylons and maximum internal fuel. The refuelling probe of the BUCCANEER is conspicuous just forward of its cockpit.

Both crew members eject successfully from a BUCCANEER S1 of 800 Squadron as it loses power seconds after launch from the waist catapult of HMS EAGLE.

The forward operating base at NANGA GAAT, Borneo, seen during the confrontation with Indonesia. Helicopters of 845, 846 and 848 Squadrons flew extensively in support of the land forces whilst disembarked from their parent carriers ALBION and BULWARK. Both WESSEX HU5 and WHIRLWIND HAS7 helicopters can be seen.

A GANNET AEW3 of 849D Flight with wheels, flaps and hook down carrying out a Carrier Controlled Approach to HMS EAGLE whilst serving with the Far East Fleet.

Seconds before launch, the FDO of HMS VIC-TORIOUS holds his green flag aloft ready to launch a BUCCANEER S2 of 801 Squadron during post-refit trials in 1966. The aircraft is tensioned in a flying attitude, the hold-back in place ready to go. It has 230 gallon slipper tanks on the inboard wing stations and live 1000 lb bombs on the outers. In his left hand the FDO holds a red flag. Should something go wrong, he will raise this to cancel the launch "losing" the green flag as he does so. The enormous 984 radar scanner with its associated IFF antenna dominates the island in the background.

The moment of launch. A BUCCANEER S2 of 801 Squadron seen leaving the starboard catapult of HMS VICTORIOUS. The strop has done its work and is falling away. The port catapult shuttle is visible in the foreground at the forward end of its travel.

A SEAVIXEN FAW2 of 893 Squadron has suffered a collapsed nose oleo whilst landing on HMS HERMES in 1968. It has managed to clear the angled deck but Jumbo the crane has had to be used to lift the aircraft in order to lash a trolley under the nose so that it can be moved more freely. It says a lot for the strength of the SEA VIXEN that it could withstand an accident such as this and be flying again within a few days.

Far East Fleet 1968. HMS HERMES carries out a replenishment at sea with RFA RELIANT to port and the RAN tanker SUPPLY to starboard. Outboard of her is HMS DIANA, a DARING class destroyer.

HMS HERMES in 1968. Aircraft visible on deck include a GANNET COD4 and GANNET AEW3s of 849A Flight. Further aft are WESSEX HAS1s of the Ship's SAR Flight and WESSEX HAS3s of 814 Squadron. SEA VIXEN FAW2s of 893 Squadron are ranged on the angled deck and right aft are BUCCANEER S2s of 801 Squadron. A WESSEX is on the after lift, spread ready for launch should it be necessary.

A WESSEX HAS3 of 814 Squadron overflying Sydney harbour during a visit to the port by HMS HERMES in 1968.

A SEA VIXEN FAW2 of 893 Squadron from HMS HERMES equipped with an air to air refuelling pod under its starboard wing offers fuel to a section of RAF LIGHTNING fighters of 74 Squadron during exercises off Singapore in 1968.

A WESSEX HU5 lifts an underslung load from HMS FEARLESS during exercises in the Mediterranean in 1969. The ability of the WESSEX to lift a section of Marines or a viable load contributed greatly to the development of amphibious warfare in the 1960s.

A WESSEX HAS3 of 814 Squadron lands between the port catapult and deck edge lift of HMS HERMES in 1969. The director is out of sight to the right but squadron maintainers are visible ahead of the aircraft with a pressure refuelling hose at the ready.

A WESSEX HAS1 of 771 Squadron from RNAS CULDROSE carries out practice SAR diver drops off the Cornish coast.

A WASP HAS1 of 829 Squadron lashed onto the diminutive flight deck of HMS NUBIAN. The wheels of the WASP are set at 45 degrees so that on being unlashed it will tend to rotate rather than slide straight over the side; a small crumb of comfort for the pilot!

A PHANTOM FG1 of 892 Squadron firing a Sidewinder heat seeking air to air missile.

A PHANTOM FG1 of 892 Squadron leaving the waist catapult of HMS ARK ROYAL. It is demonstrating its excellent attack capability with no less than thirteen 750 lb bombs on underwing pylons. Note that the strop has not fallen away into the sea; in this last example of the catapult in Royal Naval service the strop was held back for further use by the Van Zelde mechanism. Once a specified number of launches were complete it could be disconnected, discarded and replaced.

A US Navy A6E INTRUDER from VA176 Squadron is intercepted over the Mediterranean by a PHANTOM FG1 of 892 Squadron from HMS ARK ROYAL during Exercise DISPLAY DETERMINATION in 1976.

Phantom of 892 Squadron firing a salvo of 2" rockets.

A PHANTOM FG1 of 892 Squadron seconds before launch from HMS ARK ROYAL. Some idea of the size and complexity of the blast deflector, necessary to protect the rest of the deck from the thrust of the two Rolls Royce engines, can be gained. On completion of the launch, the 3 constituent parts of the deflector retract hydraulically to lie flush in their recesses in the deck.

A BUCCANEER S2 of 800 Squadron from HMS EAGLE flies low over a storm tossed sea. It is carrying its maximum conventional weapon load with four 1000 lb bombs on underwing pylons and four more in the bomb-bay. These last four were actually mounted on the reverse side of the bomb-bay door which rotated through 180 degrees to introduce them smoothly into the slipstream so that they would not tumble on being dropped.

A BUCCANEER S2 of 809 Squadron from
HMS ARK ROYAL firing a salvo of 2" rockets
from underwing pods.

The last aircraft to be launched by catapult from HMS ARK ROYAL was GANNET AEW3 XL 471, 043 of 849B Flight in November 1978. Unless the Royal Navy reverts to the use of catapults in some future carrier design, this will have been the last ever catapult launch from a British carrier.

Royal Marines of 41 Commando man WESSEX HU5 helicopters of 845
Squadron on HMS BULWARK during exercises off Scotland in 1971.

A SEA KING HAS1 of 824 Squadron lands on HMS ARK ROYAL aft whilst a GANNET AEW3 of 849B Flight, BUCCANEER S2s of 809 Squadron and PHANTOM FG1s of 892 Squadron are parked forward.

BUCCANEER leaving the waist catapult of HMS ARK ROYAL.

BUCCANEER of 801 Sqaudron over the roundown of HMS HERMES in 1969. The store under the port wing is a 2" rocket pod; that under the starboard wing, a 28lb practice bomb carrier.